MAH JONG FOR BEGINNERS

BASED ON THE RULES AND REGULATIONS
OF
THE MAH JONG ASSOCIATION
OF JAPAN

by
SHOZO KANAI
and
MARGARET FARRELL

(*Revised Edition*)

CHARLES E. TUTTLE COMPANY
RUTLAND, VERMONT & TOKYO, JAPAN

Published by the Charles E. Tuttle Company, Inc., of
Rutland, Vermont & Tokyo, Japan, with editorial
offices at Suido 1-chome, 2-6, Bunkyo-ku, Tokyo

First edition, May 1952
Second (revised) edition, January 1955
Thirty-eighth printing, 1991

Library of Congress
Catalog Card No. 58-12108

International Standard Book No. 0-8048-0391-9

Printed in Japan

Dedicated to

Mrs. M. Kanai

and

A. E. Farrell

PREFACE

MAH JONG FOR BEGINNERS

Mah Jong originated and was developed in the Orient, so the rules may seem very peculiar to Americans. In writing this book, we have used the rules and regulations of the Japan Mah Jong Association. We are indebted to Mr. Sugiura, ex-president of that association who wrote *First Steps In Mah Jong* and to Mr Hamai, president of the Osaka Yago Shoten which published his book.

At the beginning, the strategy in detail will not be shown. To do that would lead beginners into confusion because the playing is intricate. We shall try to explain from the first step, in order to be understood by those who have never seen the implements of play

Readers who desire answers to any questions concerning the playing of Mah Jong will please address their queries to the author, Shozo Kanai, in care of the publishing company.

CONTENTS

PART I. RULES AND PROCEDURE

PART II. STRATEGY

SUPPLEMENTARY

PART I.
RULES AND PROCEDURE

CHAPTER I.   HISTORY OF MAH JONG

Man Jong is the national game of China.   It is sometimes called the Chinese Game of the Four Winds.

There are many theories about its origin but none of them is valid or reliable.   It is believed that it originated from one form of card playing and during the first stage had 40 pieces, called *Pai* (pronounced pie, rhymes with lye), (in English usually called tiles, the term used in this book) which were entirely different from those of today.

Down to the 17th Century the number of tiles increased to 108.   These had the portraits of the 108 Brigands of a then-famous novel.

As time elapsed the number of tiles increased until there were more than 160, having many kinds of Bonus tiles, including Flower tiles.   Revolutionists appeared and cut down the number to make the game more interesting.   Rules and regulations were then decided and have remained the same until the present day.   The Flower tiles that we now find in the set of Mah Jong are the remains of pre-revolutionary days.

Mah Jong was imported to Japan in 1907 for the first time, and received a high reputation towards 1929.   There were many Mah Jong Clubs in every urban center and competitive games were held between Japan and China.   After the out-break of the Sino-Japanese War, Mah Jong was suppressed in due course, but on finishing the war it again caught the public fancy, multiplying by many times its former popularity.

CHAPTER II.
KIND AND NUMBER OF TILES

Tiles are usually made of bone and bamboo, but in the best quality ivory replaces the bone portion. Bone is generally derived from cattle and is imported from the U.S. and China. Bones from cattle in Japan are too small to be used in the manufacture. Plastic tiles are now being moulded to take the place of the imported bone.

There are 136 tiles in a Set. However, every Set contains another set of 4 Blanks. These are kept in reserve in case some of the tiles are lost.

There are two kinds of Letter tiles and three kinds of Numeral tiles, making up five general kinds of tiles.

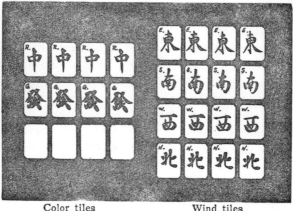

Color tiles   Wind tiles

(1)   Color Tiles
     4 - Red Letter, or Red Dragon, tiles
     4 - Green Letter, or Green Dragon, tiles

4 - Blanks (neither letter nor picture),
    called White Dragon tiles
        Total Color Tiles............................ 12

(2) Wind Tiles
    4 - East Wind tiles
    4 - South Wind tiles
    4 - West Wind tiles
    4 - North Wind tiles
        Total Wind Tiles 16
The Numeral Tiles are *Won*, Bamboo and Ball Tiles.

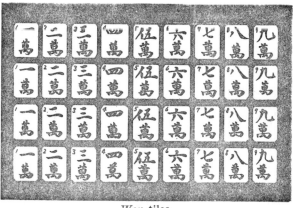

Won tiles

(3) Won Tiles (*Won* is the Chinese word for 10,000)
    1 - *Won* to 9 - *Won*, 4 of each
        Total *Won* Tiles 36
(4) Bamboo Tiles
    1 - Bamboo to 9 - Bamboo, 4 of each
        Total Bamboo Tiles 36
    (1 - Bamboo is shown with the carving of a picture
    of a bird or a bamboo shoot)

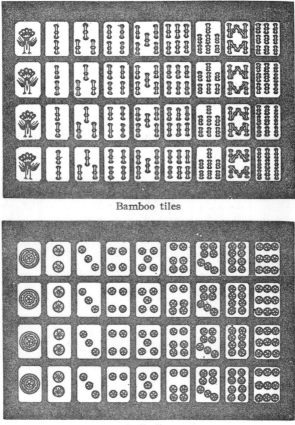

Bamboo tiles

Ball tiles

(5) Ball Tiles

　　　1 - Ball to 9 - Ball, 4 of each

　　　　　　Total Ball Tiles 36

　　　(Ball tiles are indicated by double circles)

There are other classifications

a. Old Head Tiles
   1 - *Won* and 9 - *Won*
   1 - Bamboo and 9 - Bamboo
   1 - Ball and 9 - Ball

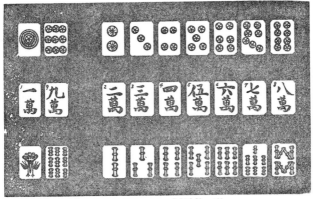

Old Head tiles   Middle tiles

b. Middle Tiles
   2 - *Won* to 8 - *Won*
   2 - Bamboo to 8 - Bamboo
   2 - Balls to 8 - Balls

c. Letter Tiles
   Color, or Dragon tiles, are often called the Three
   Original Tiles.
   Wind Tiles - East, South, West, North.
   See Illustration No.1

CHAPTER III.
DETERMINATION OF SEATS

Mah Jong is generally played by four persons. In the beginning the four players each take a seat at random. The table for playing must be square and covered with cloth having enough thickness to prevent noise.

Among the accessories of Mah Jong there are four small round discs made of bone. These have the letters of the four directions - East, South, West and North. If there are no discs, one of each of the four Wind tiles, contained in the Set, are placed upside down on the table. Then, arbitrarily, one of the players casts two dice (they also, are accessories), and counts, to the right, the number indicated by the spots on the dice, starting with himself. The seat, designated by the spots on the dice, is temporarily named the East seat.

Next, the person, in the assumed East position, throws the dice and the one, indicated by the spots, picks up the right end tile from the four reversely placed tiles (the one who made the row deciding which is the right end). Then the one who sits on the right, picks up the adjoining tile and the next does likewise.

Thus, the four players pick up the four tiles and their seats are decided by the letters on the tiles - namely, the one who picked up the East tile sits in the temporary East seat, and the one who picked up the South tile sits in the South seat and so on. In this case, the four directions are in reverse to the natural directions.

CHAPTER IV.
TO DECIDE THE ELDEST HAND

When the players' seats are decided, the Eldest Hand should be determined, The Eldest Hand is said to be the EAST HAND.

The person who took the East tile casts the dice and counts the number indicated by the spots from East (starting with himself), to the right. If the spots add up to 7, then West casts the dice next. The person, indicated by the second casting of dice, counting to the right (starting with himself) is the Eldest Hand, or East.

We can simplify the throwing of dice from twice to once, but it is more formal to throw twice.

The right hand of East is South, the opposite hand is West and the left hand is North.

When one game is over, the Eldest Hand passes to the right and South becomes East, or the Eldest Hand ; West becomes South, North becomes West and East becomes North.

CHAPTER V.
DEAL AND ARRANGEMENT OF THE TILES

Now to go ahead with the game. There are 136 tiles and they should be well mixed. Each player gathers 34 tiles to form two rows of 17 each, placing one row on top of the other. For ease in assembling the tiles it is well to remember to pick up three upside down tiles in each hand twice, then three in one hand and two in the other. This makes a row of 17. Thereafter, we can speedily pick up the other 17 tiles (All of the tiles are assembled face down).

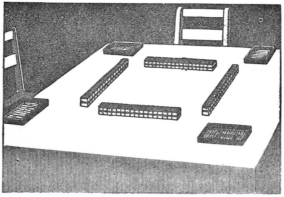

Arrangement of tiles

On finishing the arrangement, East casts the two dice to decide from where to commence to pick up the tiles. Counting the number or spots, starting with East and counting to the right, the person thus nominated casts the dice again. Adding the number of spots from both castings, and counting off that number from the right end of the nominated pile, indicates the place from which East starts taking the tiles to make up his hand.

For example, the Eldest Hand, or East, casts the dice and the spots add up to 6. The sixth player, namely South, casts dice again and the spots add up to 7. Then East takes two piles (4 tiles), EXCLUDING 13 PILES, from the right end of the row of piles in front of South. South takes the next two piles (4 tiles), then West and North take successively. Each takes thrice in order to have 12 tiles, then East takes one tile from the upper part of the pile, South takes one from the lower part and West and North take their last tile each, so that each player has 13 tiles.

There should always be 13 tiles in each hand, including melds, except in the case of :—

a. *Kan* (4 of a kind, which will be explained later)

b. Going Out and

c. Picking up from the pile.

However, East takes one more tile to make 14. To simplify the dealing, East takes two tiles successively after the four players have taken four tiles thrice.

At the beginning of the game, East has 14 tiles and the other three players have 13. These are placed upright in a line in front of each player with the bamboo backs shown to the opposite side. The 13 tiles are first placed at random in the order of picking up. Later they should be arranged in order to be easily understood. However, the arrangement should be avoided after making progress as others can guess what part is Bamboo or what part is composed of Letter tiles, when one picks up a tile for discarding or for melding. Much exercise is needed to play without arrangement.

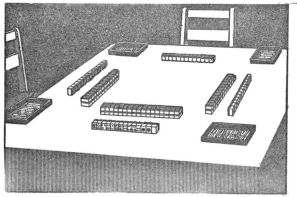

Arrangement of Hands

CHAPTER VI. HOW TO GO OUT

East, who has 14 tiles, starts the game by discarding one of his tiles. This he does by placing the discarded tile in front of his pile, facing the surface up.

Next, South picks up one tile from the end of the pile, unless he can make a *Pon* or a *Chi* (these are explained later) from the tile discarded by East. West and North pick up and discard in like manner and the play continues successively until one of the players Goes Out, or the pile is exhausted, leaving such portion as is decided by regulation.

A hand has 14 tiles when Going Out - 4 sets of threes and a pair (2 of a kind). The pair, or 2 of a kind, is called a Pillow, or Head. The threes are not gathered at random. They may be either 3 of a kind, called a *Pon*, or a sequene (run) of 3, called a *Chi*.

Pillow

There are two methods of making a *Pon* or a *Chi*.

1. When a player has two of the same kind of tiles and one of the other three players discards one of the same, he can pick up the discarded tile by saying, *"Pon"* He then melds the three tiles by placing them, surface up, to the right of his hand.

2. When a player makes a *Pon* or a *Chi* by drawing from the pile, he does not need to meld them but keeps them concealed in his hand.

In case of *Pon*, one can take from any other player's discard, but in making a *Chi*, one can take only from the left

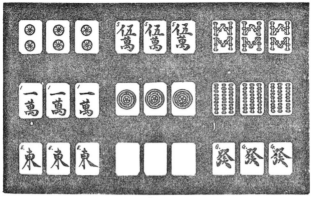

Pon

hand player's discard to complete a sequence. This difference must be remembered. The *Chi*, subsidized from the left hand, must be melded. When Going Out, however, one can complete a *Pon*, a *Chi*, or a Pillow by taking a discard from any other player.

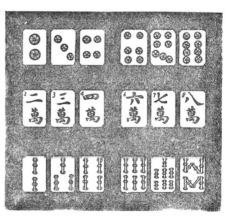

Chi

The *Pon* is mightier than the *Chi*. For example, East can make a *Pon* of 5-*Won* when South discards a 5-*Won* even though West might want it to make a *Chi*.

After East has made a *Pon* by taking the 5-*Won* discarded by South, he discards, then South again plays, not West. When

East makes a *Pon* in this way, West and North are excluded from their natural turn and West can play only after South has discarded.

Going Out is the mightiest of all. If East discards a tile that North can use to Go Out by making either a *Pon,* or a *Chi,* or a Pillow, he can pick up the discarded tile, even though South might want to use the tile to make a *Chi* and West might want it to make a *Pon*.

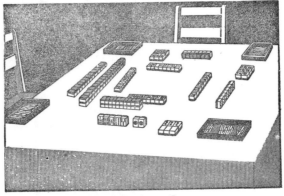

Hand Ready to Go out

CHAPTER VII.
MELD AND REMAINING TILES

In melding a *Pon,* a player must meld the 3 tiles, placing them face upward to the right of his hand to show others. However, if a player picks up the 4th tile of the same kind, he can make a meld of 4 tiles. A meld of 4 of a kind is called a *Kan* (Kawn).

A player, who has a *Pon* in his hand, can pick up a discarded tile of the same kind by saying, "*Kan*" and melding the 4 tiles. The melding of a *Kan* makes one's hand insufficient, and in order to remedy this defect one must pick an extra tile from the *far* end of the pile.

The game goes on until there are 14 tiles left. If there is no winner, that is, if none of the hands can Go Ont (leaving 14 tiles), the game is over and the Eldest Hand, or East, is changed.

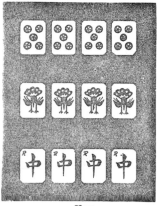

Kan

CHAPTER VIII.
ROUND WIND AND SEAT WIND

There are four rounds of play and four games in each round, unless East, or the Eldest Hand, Goes Out, in which case he will remain East until some other player wins a game.

Each round is called by the name of one of the directions. The first round is the East Wind Fight, or the East Round, the next is the South Round, then the West Round and the North Round.

In the East Round, the East tiles are always Bonus tiles, that is, any one of the four hands that has a *Pon* of East tiles in the East Round, and Goes Out, receives a Bonus. In the South Round, the South tiles are Bonus tiles, followed, in the same way, by those of West and North.

A *Pon* of the Seat Wind gives a Bonus to the player sitting in that seat, if he Goes Out. That is, if a player, sitting in the South Seat in the East Round, has a *Pon* of South tiles and Goes Out, he receives a Bonus,

When the Round Wind and the Seat Wind are the same, the *Pon* of that Wind gives a double Bonus. For example, if a player in the South Seat makes a South *Pon* during the South Round, and Goes Out, he receives a double Bonus.

The Bonuses will be explained later.

CHAPTER IX.
COUNTING THE POINTS

1. Melded *Pon* (set of 3 of a kind)   Points

   Numeral Tiles from 2- to 8- 2
     (*Won*, Bamboo or Ball)
   Wind or Color tiles 4
   1-s and 9-s.. 4

2. *Pon* in Hand (not melded) - double Melded *Pon*

   Numeral Tiles from 2- to 8. 4
   Wind or Color Tiles... 8
   1-s and 9-s 8

3. Melded *Kan* (set of 4 of a kind) - double *Pon* in Hand

   Numeral Tiles from 2- to 8- 8
   Wind or Color Tiles...16
   1-s and 9-s 16

4. *Kan* in Hand (not melded) - double Melded *Kan*

   Numeral Tiles from 2- to 8-....................................16
   Wind or Color Tiles...32
   1-s and 9-s..32

5. Pillow or Head

   Wind or Color Tiles... 2
   Double Wind Pillow 4
     Double Wind occurs when the Seat Wind and the Round Wind are the same.

6. *Chi* (sequence)

A *Chi* has no points. It is only an arrangement for Going Out.

7. For *Going Out* a player receives a *Base* of *20 Points*. The Fundamental Points (F. P.) are equal to the Base of 20 plus the sum of *Pon*, *Kan* and Pillow.

F. P. = Base + Pon + Kan + Pillow.

Bonus tile Pon(s).

A *Pon* of the Seat Wind, the Round Wind, or of Color tiles, doubles the Fundamental Points. When a player has one Bonus *Pon*, the F. P. are doubled.

(Base $20 + Pon + Kan + $ Pillow) $\times 2$

When a player has three Bonus *Pon(s)*, the F. P. are doubled three times. (Base $20 + 3$ Pons + Pillow) $\times 2 \times 2 \times 2$(or $\times 8$).

The above cases refer to the points in the hand, but the following four cases apply only in Going Out.

Points

(1) When one Goes Out by making a pillow 2

(2) When one Goes Out by completing a *Chi* by filling in an Intermediate tile 2

For example :—Completing a 4 - 5 - 6 Ball *Chi* by getting a 5 - Ball tile.

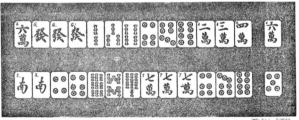

Going Out by making a Pillow
Going Out with an Intermediate

(3) When one Goes Out by completing a *Chi* with a
 Marginal tile 2

For example :—7 - *Won* is the Marginal tile of the 7 - 8 - 9 -
Won Chi. A 3 - Ball tile is the Marginal tile of the 1 - 2 -3 -
Ball *Chi.*

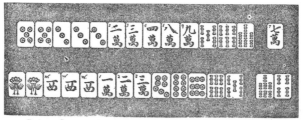

Going Out with a Marginal tile
This hand can Go Out with either a 4-Bamboo tile
 or with a 7-Bamboo tile

(4) When one Goes Out with a tile drawn from the
 pile 2

For example :—with the above hand a player has two chances
to Go Out. It he Goes Out by drawing either a 4 - Bamboo
or a 7 - Bamboo from the pile he gets 2 points.

The above points in Nos. 1, 2, and 3 are doubled if a
player picks a tile from the pile to make up the pillow to Go
Out, or if he picks an Intermediate or a Marginal tile from
the pile to Go Out.

If during the South Round, one of the players Goes Out by
making a pillow of South tiles by picking up from the pile, he
gets a total of 6 points.

Pillow of South tiles 2
Going Out by making a Pillow................................. 2
Going Out by drawing from the pile........................... 2
  Total.................. 6

If a player in the South Seat, during the South Round,

makes a Pillow of South tiles by picking up from the pile and Goes Out, he gets 8 points.

Pillow of South tiles 4
Going Out by making a Pillow................................ 2
Going Out by drawing from the pile......................... 2

Total.................. 8

Great care must be taken in counting the points because many times they overlap.

The before-mentioned points are the points in the hand, but the following points are the Bonuses for Going Out.

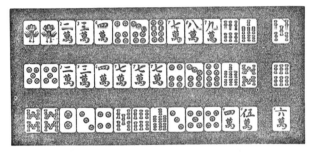

Four *Chis* and Pillow (no Letter tiles)
Numeral tiles 2- to 8- only ; *Pon*, or *Chi* and Pillow
Numeral tiles 2- to 8- only, but having four *Chis.*

Bonuses for Going Out

1. Hand has 4 *Chi* (s) and Pillow (no Letter tiles) and Goes Out with a discarded tile............F. P. or Base × 2
   (Letter tiles are the Wind and Color tiles)
   There are no extra points in this hand, so the Fundamental Points are the Base of 20 only.
2. Hand has only Numeral tiles 2- to 8- (*Pon* or *Chi*) F. P. × 2
   This hand has no 1-s or 9-s or Letter tiles.
   The Numeral tiles may be *Won*, Bamboo and Ball.

3. Hand has 4 *Chi(s)* Numeral tiles 2- to 8- only......F. P. × 4
This hand has no 1-s or 9-s or Letter tiles.

All Bamboo

4. (a) Hand has only ONE kind of Numeral tiles......F. P. × 8
This hand must be all *Won*, or all Bamboo, or all Balls,
including the Pillow.

All *Won*, no 1-s or 9-s

(b) If above hand has no 1-s or 9-s...............F. P. × 16
5. (a) If a hand Goes Out without melding............F. P. × 2
This is called a concealed hand.

Player must pick up ALL of the tiles from the pile.

(b) If a player picks up a discarded tile to Go Out,
without having melded and having no other Bonus...F P. + 10
No multiplication.

Letter tiles and one kind of Numeral tiles

6. Hand composed of Letter tiles and ONE kind of
Numeral tiles ....F. P. × 2
Letter tiles are Wind or Color tiles.

Numeral tiles may be *Won*, or Bamboo, or Balls.

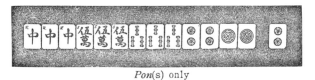

Pon(s) only

7. Hand composed of *Pon* (s) only .... F P. × 2
Pon (s) include both melded and concealed *Kan* (s).

Three Concealed *Pon*(s)

8. (a) Hand has 3 concealed *Pon*(s), *Kan*(s) included
....F. P. × 2
  (b) If the above hand Goes Out with a melded *Pon*
or *Kan*, besides the 3 concealed *Pon* (s) ....F. P. × 4
  (c) If the above concealed hand Goes Out by drawing
from the pile...F. P. × 4
  (d) If the above concealed hand Goes Out with a discarded
tile the F. P. are doubled only according to the value of
the *Pon* (☒).

9. Hand has NO Numeral tiles from 2- to 8-.........F. P. × 2
The points in this hand are comparatively large because the
1-s and 9-s and the Letter tiles have double the value of the others.

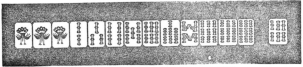

Dragon tiles for two *Pon*(s) and Pillow

10. Hand has Color tiles, or Dragon tiles, for 2 *Pon* (s) and the Pillow ....F. P. × 8
Color tiles are Bonus tiles.

11. When a player Goes Out with a tile which supplements the one used to make up a *Kan* ....F. P. × 2
This is called, " Opening a Flower on the Top of the Mountain."

12. When a player Goes Out by taking the very last tile (excluding the 14 remaining tiles) ....F. P. × 2
This is called, " Taking up the Moon from the Bottom of the Sea".

13. When the last tile is taken up and discarded, if one of the other players can use the discarded tile to Go Out, his points are doubled ....F. P. × 2
This is called, " Taking up the Fish from the Bottom of the River ".

One player has melded a *Pon* of 6-Balls. He draws the fourth 6-Ball tile to make a *Kan*. However, another hand is *Tempai*(ed), waiting for a 6-Ball or a 9-Ball, so the instant the former makes a *Kan*, the latter says " Out ". The 6-Ball tile completes his hand and doubles his points.

14. When a player Goes Out with a tile drawn by another player to make up a melded *Kan* ....F. P. × 2

(The player, who can Go Out, is permitted to do this).

15. *Rhichi*

After the 14 tiles are dealt and the one which is not needed is discarded, if the Eldest Hand, or East, discovers that he needs only one tile to complete his hand, he says, " *Rhichi* ", then if he Goes Out his points are doubled ....F. P. × 2

The hand must not be changed, after the declaration, by any tile drawn from the pile.

The other three players may declare " *Rhichi* " after they have drawn and discarded the first tile. They also may not change their hands after the declaration.

Recently the rule about " *Rhichi* " has been changed to permit any player to declare " *Rhichi* " at any time after his hand has been completed, except for one tile.

If he Goes Out after declaring "*Rhichi* "............F. P. × 2

After declaring "*Rhichi* ", a player usually turns his hand face downward on the table until such time as he can draw the lucky tile.

Three *Chi*(s) of one kind of Numeral
Seven Pairs

16. When a hand is composed of a sequence of 3 *Chi*(s) of one kind of Numeral (*Won*, Bamboo or Balls)......F. P. × 2

For example :—1 - 2 - 3 -;   4 - 5 - 6 -;   7 - 8 - 9 -;

but not overlapping, such as, 1 - 2 - 3 - ;   3 - 4 - 5 - ;   5 - 6 - 7 -.

Bonus hands are often doubled and redoubled, so great care must be taken in counting the points.

17.   A hand that contains 7 pairs can Go Out. If the Eldest Hand, or East, Goes Out with 7 pairs, he gets 600 points (200 from each of the other players).

If one of the other players Goes Out with 7 pairs, he gets 400 points, (200 points from East and 100 from each of the others.

CHAPTER X.
MAXIMUM LIMIT OF POINTS

There are many Bonuses and points which are multiplied very often so that sometimes the total points increase to some five hundred thousand, or a million.

When one gets such points, or when one must pay such points, the game becomes uninteresting.   Therefore a limit is set.

By Bonus Regulations, a limit of 3000 points is set for the Eldest Hand, or East, and a limit of 2000 points for the other players.

However, there are some hands which can get the maximum points even though the actual counting points do not amount to the limit of 2000 or 3000.

1.   The Eldest Hand, or East, takes 14 tiles at first.
If he can Go Out with these tiles he gets .... max. pts.

This is called, " The Going Out of the Gods ".

2.   When South, West, or North Goes Out by taking the first tile discarded by East, he gets .... max. pts.

3.   Going Out by using the three kinds of Color, or Dragon tiles .... max. pts.

3 *Pon*(s) of the 3 dragon tiles are needed.

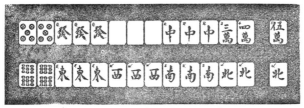

Three *Pon*(s) of three Dragon tiles
Four *Pon*(s) of four Wind tiles

4. Going Out by using the 4 *Pon*(s) of the 4 Winds.
.... max. pts.
   3 Wind *Pon*(s) and a Pillow of Wind tiles also gives
   .... max. pts.

All 1-s and 9-s

5. Going Out with a hand in which all the *Pon*(s) and
the Pillow are 1-s and 9-s ....max. pts.

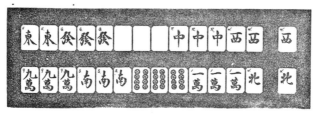

Letter tiles only
Four Concealed *Pon*(s)

6. Going Out with a hand composed of Letter tiles only
.... max. pts.

(Letter tiles are Wind and Color tiles).

7. Going Out with 4 concealed *Pon*(s) ....max. pts.
Melded *Pon*(s) or *Kan*(s) are not allowed.

(3 concealed *Pon*(s) doubles the F. P. - see "*Pon* in Hand" in paragraph 2. COUNTING THE POINTS).

8. Going Out with 3 *Kan*(s), either melded or concealed, is sometimes allowed the maximum points, but usually this hand is limited to ....F. P. × 2

9. Going Out with 4 *Kan*(s) in the hand ....max. pts.

4 *Kan* (s) are difficult to make, but if more than one player can make 4 *Kan* (s) , the game is over and no count is allowed.

Pon(s) of 1-s and 9-s plus a Sequence

10. Going Out with a hand composed of one *Pon* of 1-s and one *Pon* of 9-s plus a sequence of 2 - 3 - 4 - 5 - 6 - 7 - 8 -
.... max. pts.

(The sequence may be any kind or all one kind of Numeral) . When a player has 13 tiles arranged as above he has 9 chances to Go Out. Any Numeral from 1- to 9- will make a Pillow to Go Out. This hand must be concealed.

One of each of the four Wind tiles and three Dragon tiles, and one of each of the 1-s and 9-s of the three kinds of Numeral tiles

11. A hand that has one of each of the 4 Wind tiles and 3 Color tiles, and one of each of the 1-s and 9-s of the 3 kinds

of Numeral tiles, has 13 chances to Go Out by drawing any one of those tiles to make up a Pillow ....max. pts.

Usually this hand has a Pillow and only waits for the missing 14th.

12. When the Eldest Hand, or East, Goes Out, that player remains the Eldest Hand for another game. In case the Eldest Hand should Go Out 8 successive times, he will receive the maximum points on the 9th game, even though the Fundamental Points are only 22, with no multiplication.

CHAPTER XI. NO WINNING

No Winning is called *Pin-Chui*. There are four cases.

1. When no player has Gone Out and the tiles are exhausted, (leaving the 14 tiles), the game is over and the next player, or South, becomes the Eldest Hand, or East.

2. When a player has been dealt more than 9 different kinds of tiles, including 1-s and 9-s and Letter tiles, he can claim " No Game ". The Eldest Hand must declare " No Game " after he has picked up the first 14 tiles. The other players must declare " No Game " immediately after they have drawn the first tile from the pile. However, a player is not obliged to say " No Game " with the above hand. He can try to make up a maximum hand. See paragraphs 10 and 11 in " Maximum Limit of Points ".

3. When the same kind of Wind tiles are discarded in the first round of the game by all four players, the game is over and the next hand, South, becomes the Eldest Hand, or East.

4. When more than one player makes four *Kan*(s), the game is over. When the second player makes a fourth *Kan*, the game ends and no count is allowed.

CHAPTER XII. PENALTIES

1. When a player makes a mistake and declares he is **Going Out** with a hand which cannot Go Out, that player must pay half of the maximum points.

For example, if the Eldest Hand, or East, makes the mistake, he pays 1500 points (500 to each of the other players). If one of the other players makes the mistake, he pays 1000 **points** (500 to East and 250 to each of the others). However, if the other players do not show their hands, the one who had made the mistake need not pay.

This rule is in effect only after the other players have shown their hands.

2. If a player makes a mistake in melding a *Chi* or a *Pon*, that player cannot Go Out. However, if the mistake is corrected before the next player draws from the pile, there is no penalty.

3. When a player says, " *Pon* " without two more of the same kind as the discarded tile, he must pay 100 points to the winner of that game. Even if he has two of the same kind and does not meld after saying " *Pon* ", he must pay 100 points.

4. When a player does not have 13 tiles in his hand, or if he has more than 13, through some carelessness, he cannot Go Out.

5. At times, certain tiles should not be discarded. For example, one player has melded three Numeral *Pon*(s) or *Chi*(s) of the same kind of Numeral tiles. One of the other players discards a Numeral tile which the first player uses to make a fourth *Pon* or *Chi* and Goes Out by drawing from the pile. Normally, the player who went out would be paid by the other three players, but in this case, the player who made the discard and made the Going Out possible, must pay the total. This is

due to the fact that the hand that went out, had already shown three melds, and the danger of this hand Going Out, having only one kind of tile, could be easily perceived. Yet the player, who discarded, dared to disregard the danger and gave the first player the opportunity to Go Out. If the other two players had to pay equally for the misdoing of the third, that would not be fair. Thus this regulation was established.

(a) When there are 3 melds of the same kind of Numeral tiles, those Numeral tiles should not be discarded (stated above).

(b) When 2 *Pon*(s) of the three Color tiles have been melded, the tile of the third Color should not be discarded.

(c) When 3 *Pon* (s) of the Wind tiles have been melded, the tile of the fourth Wind should not be discarded.

(d) When 3 *Pon* (s) of the Letter tiles (Wind and Color) have been melded, a Letter tile should not be discarded.

(e) When 3 *Pon* (s) of the 1-s and 9-s have been melded, the 1-s and 9-s should not be discarded.

Players holding the above hands are waiting to get the maximum points. The intention is easily recognized, so the other hands ally themselves to prevent the dangerous hand from Going Out. When one player breaks the treaty, he must pay all the points as the penalty. We think this is a good rule.

CHAPTER XIII.
EXERCISES IN GOING OUT

Fourteen tiles for East and 13 for each of the other three hands are dealt as follows :—

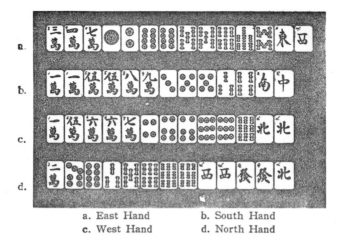

a. East Hand   b. South Hand
c. West Hand   d. North Hand

a. Looking at East's hand first. It already has a complete sequence, 6-7-8-Bamboo. They make up a *Chi* and should be kept intact. Besides the sequence, or *Chi*, there are two 5-Bamboo tiles and two 5-Ball tiles, which may be used to make up *Pon* (s) (three of a kind). The 3-4-*Won* and the 1-2-Balls may be used for *Chi* (s). If we complete two *Chi* (s) and one *Pon*, plus a Pillow (2 of a kind), we can Go Out. Therefore, the remaining East tile, West tile and 7-*Won* are not needed.

b. Let us look at the hand of South. There are two 1-*Won* (s), two 5-*Won* tiles and two 5-Ball tiles for *Pon* (s). The 8-9 *Won* and the 3-4-Bamboo are germs for *Chi* (s). If a 4-Ball tile is drawn, a *Chi* may be made with the 3-Ball and one of the 5-Balls. The other 5-Ball may then be discarded. The South tile and the Red Dragon tile are not necessary and may also be discarded.

c. Next is the West hand. It has two North tiles and two 9-Ball tiles. The 4-Ball and the two 6-Ball tiles can be used to make up either a *Chi* or a *Pon*. The 5-*Won*, the two

— 28 —

6-*Won* tiles and the 7-*Won* make a complete *Chi*, excluding one 6-*Won*, but they can also be treated to make up two *Chi* (s), using the 5-*Won* and the 6-*Won* together, and the 6-*Won* and the 7-*Won*.

d. The last is North's hand. This has two Green Dragons, two West tiles, 7-8-Balls, and 5-6-Bamboo. The 7-8-Balls and the 5-6-Bamboo may be used to make up two *Chi* (s).

Finishing the inspection of the four hands, let us start the game.

The East hand is the Eldest Hand and must discard one tile out of the 14. He has a choice of three discards-the East tile, the West tile, or the 7-*Won*. Since this is the East Seat and the East Wind Round, the East tile should be cherished. The 7-*Won* may possibly be used in a sequence, or *Chi*, if an adjoining tile is drawn, so in this case the West tile should be discarded.

Ordinarily, South would take a tile from the pile, but North has two West tiles so he takes the West tile, discarded by East, loudly saying, " *Pon* ". He places the three West tiles on the table, surface up, to the right of his hand. Before arranging the three tiles making up a *Pon* or a *Chi*, a player must be careful to make a discard. North discards 2-*Won*.

Again, East has a turn (South and West having been excluded from their natural turn because of North's *Pon*). East has 3-4-*Won*. He wants a 2-*Won*, so he picks up North's discard and completes a *Chi*. Before taking up the 2-*Won*, he discards a 7-*Won*, then makes up the *Chi* to the right of his hand.

South has the next turn. He has 8-9-*Won* so he takes the 7-*Won*, discarded by East, to complete a *Chi*. South discards a Red Dragon and melds the *Chi* to the right.

West does not need the Red Dragon so draws a tile from the pile. It is a 5-Ball and completes a *Chi* of 4-5-6-Balls.

— 29 —

Since West completes a *Chi* in his hand he does not need to meld it. West discards a 9-Bamboo.

North again says, " *Pon* ", discards a 3-Bamboo, and melds his *Pon* of 9-Bamboo tiles.

East does not need the 3-Bamboo, so draws from the pile. This is a White Dragon, which he discards.

South then draws from the pile. He draws a 5-*Won* and completes a *Pon* in his hand. This does not need to be melded. South discards a South tile, even though it is his Seat Wind.

West draws from the pile. He draws an 8-Bamboo which has no connection in his hand. However, he keeps it in reserve and discards 1-*Won*. " *Pon* ", loudly says South and discards a 3-Ball tile. South melds the 1-*Won Pon* and is now ready to Go Out if he gets either a 2-Bamboo or a 5-Bamboo tile.

A hand arranged to Go Out by getting only one more tile is called " *Tembai* ".

West draws a tile. It is an 8-Bamboo. Then West has two 8-Bamboo tiles. He discards a 6-Ball tile.

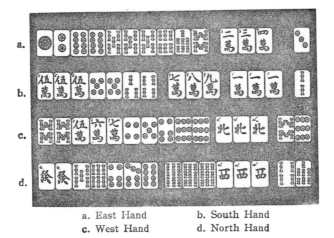

a. East Hand

c. West Hand

b. South Hand

d. North Hand

North says, "*Chi*", discards a North tile, and melds 6-7-8-Balls. West makes a *Pon* of the North discard, and discards 6-*Won*. He can now Go Out by getting either 8-Bamboo or a 9-Ball tile.

North draws a White Dragon, which he discards. North's hand needs only a 4-Bamboo or 7-Bamboo. East draws a 5-Bamboo from the pile and completes a *Pon* in his hand. He then discards his East tile.

All of the four hands are ready to Go Out. Now let us count the points when each Goes Out.

Points

a. East - Melded *Chi* of 2-3-4-*Won* 0
        Pon in Hand (concealed), three 5 Bamboo tiles......4
        For Going Out with 3-Ball tile (if discarded) 2
                              (if drawn) 4

When the hand Goes Out with a discarded tile, the Fundamental Points are 26 (Base $20 + 4 + 2$). The 26 points are doubled for the Eldest Hand, or East - $26 \times 2 = 52$. (52 is cut pay down to 50). The player, who discarded the 3-Ball tile, must pay $50 \times 3 = 150$. The other two hands do not need to pay, since the one who discarded pays for them.

When the Eldest Hand, or East, Goes Out by itself, that is, by drawing a tile from the pile, to complete his hand, the Fundamental Points are doubled - $28 \times 2 = 56$. (56 is raised to 60). In this case each of the other three hands pays East 60 points-total 180 points.

    (46 to 54 points pay 50)
    (56 to 64 points pay 60)

Points

b. South - Melded *Chi*, 7-8-9-*Won* 0
        Melded *Pon*, three 1-*Won* tiles 4
        Pon in Hand (concealed), three 5-*Won* tiles......4

Going Out with 2-Ball, or 5-Ball (if discarded) ...0

(if drawn) 2

When South Goes Out by picking up a discarded tile, the Fundamental Points are 28 (Base $20+4+4$), and the player who discarded must pay South $30 \times 4 = 120$ points. (60 points for East and 30 for each of the other two hands).

When South Goes Out by itself, that is, by drawing a tile from the pile to complete his hand, East must pay $30 \times 2 = 60$. West and North must pay 30 points, respectively.

The Eldest Hand, or East, must always pay, or be paid, double. The one, whose discarded tile completes the Going Out of the Eldest Hand, must pay six times the Fundamental Points ($3 \times 2 = 6$). When hands, other than the Eldest, or East Hand, Go Out by a discarded tile, the hand which discarded, must pay four times the Fundamental Points, that is, twice (or double) the sum of the Fundamental Points for the Eldest Hand, or East, and the sum of the Fundamental Points for each of the other two hands.

Points

c. West - Melded *Pon* of 3 North tiles 4

    a. Going Out with *Pon* of 8-Bamboo

        and Pillow of 9-Balls ....2 by discard (1)

                           4 if drawn (2)

    b. Going Out with *Pon* of 9-Balls

        and Pillow of 8-Bamboo ......4 by discard (3)

                           6 if drawn (4)

Fundamental Points

(1) $20+4+2 = 26$

Player, who discarded, pays $30 \times 4 = 120$

(2) $20+4+4 = 28$

Eldest Hand pays $30 \times 2 = 60$

Other two hands pay 30 each

(3) $20+4+4=28$
    Player, who discarded, pays $30 \times 4 = 120$
(4) $20+4+6=30$
    Eldest Hand pays $30 \times 2 = 60$
    Other two hands pay 30 each

d.   North - Melded *Pon* of West tiles 4
            Melded *Pon* of 9-Bamboo 4
            Melded *Chi*, 6-7-8-Balls 0
            Pillow, Green Dragon 2
            Going Out with 4- or 7-Bamboo...0 by discard (1)
                                              2 if drawn (2)

    Fundamental Points
(1) $20+4+4+2=30$
    Player, who discarded, pays $30 \times 4 = 120$
(2) $20+4+4+2+2=32$
    East pays 60
    Other hands pay 30 each

The above examples show how to Go Out and how to calculate points.   When there are Bonuses, the Fundamental Points are multiplied.

CHAPTER XIV.
EXAMPLES IN COUNTING

In the playing of Mah Jong, the intricate rules and regulations require the careful counting of the points.   Several examples in counting are given here.   Please read and practice these examples.

Example 1.

Example 1.

Assuming that the West hand Goes Out with 7-Bamboo, discarded by South, let us count the points of this hand.

Fundamental Points :— Points

Pon of 1-*Won* (melded) 4

Pon of Green Dragon (concealed) 8

Base 20

Total F. P. 32

Then the Fundamental Points are doubled, $32 \times 2 = 64$, because the Green Dragon is one of the Bonus tiles. The hand which discarded, namely South, must pay its own share of 60 points plus that of the other two hands. North's share is 60 points, the same as South's, but that of East, the Eldest Hand, is doubled, $64 \times 2 = 128$, or 130 points. So South, the hand which discarded the 7-Bamboo, must pay 60 for himself, 60 for North and 130 for East, making a total of 250 points.

When the Eldest Hand, or East, Goes Out with a tile discarded by one of the other hands, having a hand similar to the above example, the player who discarded must pay 390 points. The Fundamental Points of 64 are doubled for the Eldest Hand, $64 \times 2 = 130$. Each of the other players must pay 130, making a total of $130 \times 3 = 390$ points.

If the West Hand Goes Out by drawing the 7-Bamboo from the pile, the Fundamental Points are much more than in the former case, that is 2 more points are added to the former Fundamental Points. Then the F. P. are 34. This, doubled by the Bonus *Pon* of the Green Dragon, is $34 \times 2 = 68$, or 70 points. Since the Eldest Hand must pay double, as well as get double, he pays $68 \times 2 = 136$, or 140 points. Therefore, West receives a total of 280 points - 70 from South, 70 from North and 140 from East.

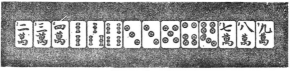

Example 2.

Example 2.

All in the hand - Concealed.

When South discards 7-*Won* and North Goes Out, with the above hand, by taking the discarded tile, how many points does the North hand get ?

Points

For completing a *Chi* with a Marginal tile............... 2

Extra points for Going Out with a discarded tile without having melded previously.............................10

(see " Bonus for Going Out ", paragraph 5. b.)

Base 20

Total F. P.   32

For South and West - $32 \times 2 = 64$, or 60 points for both.   For East (who always pays double) - $32 \times 2 = 64$, or 60 points. Therefore South must pay 120 points to North.   When North Goes Out, with the same hand, by drawing 7-*Won* from the pile, how many points does each hand have to pay ?

For drawing a Marginal tile to make a *Chi* 2

For drawing from the pile to Go Out 2

Base 20

Total F. P.   24

If the above hand Goes Out with a concealed hand, the points are doubled - $24 \times 2 = 48$ points.   Then the South and West hands must pay 50 points each, and the Eldest Hand, or East, must pay $48 \times 2 = 96$, or 100 points.

Comparing the two cases, it can be easily understood that a concealed hand gives many more points, so melds should be avoided, if possible.

Now, count the points made by the Eldest Hand, or East, when he Goes Out with the same hand, either by a discard, or by drawing the 7-*Won.*

Answer :— Going Out with a discarded tile, East gets F. P. $32 \times 2 = 64$, or 60 points from each of the other three players. $60 \times 3 = 180$ points.

Going Out by drawing from the pile, East gets F. P. 24×2 (because the hand is concealed) $\times 2$ (because his is the Eldest Hand) $= 96$, or 100 points. Therefore, the other three hands must pay 100 points each. $100 \times 3 = 300$ points.

Example 3.

Example 3.

If the Eldest Hand, or East, Goes Out by getting a discarded 5-Bamboo to complete the above hand, he gets the following points :—

	Points
Melded *Pon* of the Green Dragon	4
Melded *Pon* of the Red Dragon	4
Concealed *Pon* of 3-Balls	4
For the Intermediate 5-Bamboo, completing a *Chi*	2
Base	20
Total F. B.	34

Both the Green Dragon and the Red Dragon are Bonus tiles, and the player is the Eldest Hand, or East, therefore the 34 is multiplied by 8 $(2 \times 2 \times 2)$. $34 \times 8 = 272$, or 270 points. So the hand, which discarded the 5-Bamboo, must pay $270 \times 3 = 810$ points to East.

When one of the other hands (not East) Goes Out, under the above conditions, he gets 550 points from the player who discarded.

Fundamental Points—34

Bonus *Pon*(s) of Green Dragon and Red Dragon —

$34 \times 2 \times 2 = 136$, or 140 points.

The Eldest Hand, or East, pays $136 \times 2 = 272$, or 270 points.
The other two hands pay 140 each. $140 \times 2 = 280$ points.
Total $270 + 280 = 550$ points.

If the Eldest Hand, or East, Goes Out by drawing from the pile, he gets 290 points from each of the other hands, because the Fundamental Points are 36. $36 \times 2 \times 2 \times 2 = 288$, or 290. Total $290 \times 3 = 870$ points.

If one of the other hands Goes Out by drawing from the pile, he gets 290 (F. P. $36 \times 2 \times 2 \times 2 = 288$, or 290) from East, and 140 (F. P. $36 \times 2 \times 2 = 144$, or 140) from each of the other two hands. Total $290 + 140 + 140 = 570$ points.

Assuming that the Eldest Hand, or one of the other hands, Goes Out with a concealed hand, how many points does he get ?

Answer :— If the Eldest Hand draws the 5-Bamboo from the pile to Go Out, the Fundamental Points are 44.

Points

Concealed *Pon* of the Green Dragon	8
Concealed *Pon* of the Red Dragon	8
Concealed *Pon* of 3-Balls	4
Going Out with Intermediate 5-Bamboo tile	2
Going Out by drawing from the pile	2
Base	20
Total F. P.	44

The 44 points are multiplied by 8 $(2 \times 2 \times 2)$, because both the Green Dragon and the Red Dragon are Bonus tiles and the hand was concealed. $44 \times 2 \times 2 \times 2 = 352$, or 350 points. 352

is doubled for the Eldest Hand—$352 \times 2 = 704$, or 700 points. Therefore, East gets 700 points from each of the others. $700 \times 3 = 2100$ points.

If one of the other players Goes Out he gets 1400 points. East pays double—$350 \times 2 = 700$ points, other players pay 350 each. Total $700 + 350 + 350 = 1400$ points.

If the West hand Goes Out by using a discarded 4-Bamboo tile, he gets the following poinis.

Points

Melded Green Dragon *Pon*	4
Melded Red Dragon *Pon*	4
Concealed *Pon* of 3-Balls	4
Base	20
Total F. P.	32

The Fundamental Points are multiplied by 4, due to the Bonus tiles of the Green Dragon and the Red Dragon. $32 \times 4 = 128$, or 130 points. South and North each pay 130 points—$130 \times 2 = 260$ points. East pays double—$130 \times 2 = 260$ points. Therefore, the hand which discarded pays West—520 points.

If the Eldest Hand, or East, Goes Out, he will receive F. P. $32 \times 4 \times 2 \times 256$, or 260 from each of the other three players. Total $260 \times 3 = 780$ points.

CHAPTER XV. FLOWER TILES

In the history of Mah Jong we referred to the eight Flower tiles. Now we shall explain how to use them.

In the early days, when the playing of Mah Jong was first introduced into Japan, the Flower tiles were used by all players. Soon after, however, they lost their favor among Mah Jong lovers, because drawing such a Bonus tile which doubled the points of the hand Going Out was considered too lucky, as compared with others, who must use great skill and technique to build up a Bonus hand according to the intricate Bonus Rules. Therefore, the Flower tiles were esteemed to hinder the technical progress in making up good hands, and now the Flower tiles are seldom used.

Strictly speaking, the name Flower tile is not correct, because they are composed of two kinds, namely, four Flower and four Seasonal tiles.

The four Flower tiles are Orchid, Bamboo, Chrysanthemum and Plum. The four Seasonal tiles are Spring, Summer, Autumn and Winter. These also correspond to the four directions.

For example :— Spring, Orchid, East
Summer, Bamboo, South
Autumn, Chrysanthemum, West
Winter, Plum, North

When we use these tiles, we mix them up with the other tiles, but when we make up the four hands, we make up eighteen double piles, instead of seventeen.

The game is played in the ordinary way, except when a player draws one of these tiles.

When one draws a Flower tile, he puts it at the side, like a meld, and draws a tile from the very last pile to supplement it in his hand, in the same way as when one melds a *Kan.* If two or more Flower tiles are drawn, a player draws a supplementary tile each time from the end of the pile after he melds it, that is, places it face up to the right of his hand.

Each Flower tile (or Seasonal tile) adds 4 points to the Fundamental Points of the hand which Goes Out.

However, if a player has a Flower tile, which corresponds to his Seat or the Round Wind and Goes Out, his Fundamental Points are doubled.

For instance, in the South Round, if East has Fundamental

Points of 28 plus an Orchid tile, he has 4 more points added to his Fundamental Points, making a total of 32 points- Then, because the Orchid tile corresponds to his Seat Wind, the Fundamental Points are doubled—32×2, making a total of 64 points.

If this occurs in the East Round that East melds an Orchid tile, his Fundamental Points are doubled twice, $32 \times 2 \times 2 = 128$.

Having melded both an Orchid tile and Spring tile, and Going Out in the East Round, East would have 8 points added to the Fundamental Points of 28, making a total of $28 + 8 = 36$ points. The 36 points would then be doubled twice by the Orchid tile and twice by the Spring tile, $26 \times 2 \times 2 \times 2 \times 2 = 288$ points.

If a Set, that is, four of either kind of Flower or Seasonal tiles are drawn, and a player who has them Goes Out, he receives the Maximum points.

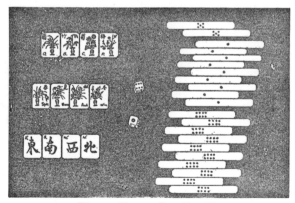

Flower tiles   Counting Bars

CHAPTER XVI. COUNTING BARS

Counting Bars are illustrated here.

They are accessories in the Mah Jong Sets, the same as the dice. There are 8 Bars which represent 500 points each, 36 Bars which represent 100 points each and 40 Bars which represent 10 points each.

The 500-point Bars are often called the Flags of the Regiment because they are very precious.

Although the markings on the Bars may vary in different Sets, the number and values are always the same.

At the start of the Game, each player has :—

two 500-point Bars,

nine 100-point Bars and

ten 10-point Bars

making a total of 2000 points.

This amount corresponds to the Maximum Points, not of the Eldest Hand, but of the other hands.

The losers of each game pay the winner by using these Bars. When the last game of the North (or last) Round is over, every player counts his Bars to decide whether he wins or loses.

PART II.
STRATEGY

There are 13 or 14 tiles in each hand and although every one has a different face as compared with others, each has certain features or characteristics.

When a player inspects his hand after the tiles have been dealt and arranged, he will have to decide how to play the hand. With practice, a player will be able to determine this at a glance. To achieve this technique, however, one must master the most fundamental and general principles of strategy.

As was previously referred to in earlier Chapters, we examine our hands when the 13 or 14 tiles are dealt and count the number of pairs (twos of a kind) and serial tiles. When we have more than four pairs, we can expect to Go Out. In cases such as this, we count how many chances we have to complete our hand, ready to Go Out on getting the fourteenth. The chances to complete our hand, ready to Go Out, are the most important issues in playing Mah Jong.

When a player needs four chances to draw tiles from the pile he can reasonably expect, or intend, to Go Out. But, precisely speaking, the tiles, which are drawn in due time, are the deciding factor. When more than five chances are needed, a hand can scarcely hope to Go Out. If a hand needs five chances, when the requisite tiles are ideally drawn, it generally takes nine or ten, and in worse cases, more than thirteen draws, before a player can supplement the required five tiles. If one dares to attempt to complete his hand by discarding dangerous tiles which are not needed in his hand, others, who are deliberately and carefully completing their hands, will be given chances to Go Out.

Having given up the intention to Go Out, a player must try not to give the chance to Go Out to hands that may have many Bonuses. One should try not to discard desirable 3-, 4-, 5- and 6-Numeral tiles and should try to keep Bonus tiles, to prevent others from making up Bonus *Pon*(s). We must note that to give up the intention to Go Out is one of the most important tactics and techniques in the game.

In general, one who can Go Out early completes his hand, ready to Go Out, after drawing eight or nine times (making a meld of a *Pon* or *Chi*, is counted as a draw), and can expect to Go Out on the twelfth or thirteenth draw. Therefore, one must always keep this in mind and discard carefully after several rounds of play. However, we perceive the fact that our hands sometimes change to good, or to bad, according to the tiles that are drawn. At times we may be lucky in drawing Intermediate or Marginal tiles which improve our hand sufficiently so that we may be able to Go Out with a concealed hand.

It also happens at times that none of the four hands are able to Go Out after thirteen or fourteen rounds of play. Then we may try to complete our hand, ready to Go Out, by daring to discard a dangerous tile, though we may have refrained from such a desire earlier, having a poor hand and not wishing to give another hand a chance to Go Out with our discard.

CHAPTER I.
HOW TO DEAL WITH THE WIND TILES
OF THE OTHER HANDS

In starting a game, the tiles which are not needed are discarded. The Wind tiles which are not the Round tiles or the Seat tiles, are usually discarded early. This is due to the fact that the Wind *Pon*(s) of other hands give only 4 points (and only 8 points even when concealed). These Wind *Pon*(s) do not have such great Bonus values. For instance, a hand that is composed of only Numeral tiles from 2- to 8- (that is, no 1-s or 9-s or Letter tiles), is a Bonus hand and one that is easy to make. If we wish to complete Bonus hands which have only Letter tiles and one kind of Numeral tiles, or Maximum hands composed of Letter tiles only, then we may keep a Wind tile and wait, hoping to draw another. When we have no such intention, it is better to discard the Wind tiles as soon as possible, before some other hand, which corresponds to the Wind tile, has a chance to draw two and can make up a Bonus *Pon* using our discard.

The above is the rule when we have only one Wind tile. Then what shall we do when we have two ?

We can keep them to use as a Pillow or to make up a *Pon*. But it is not advisable to make a *Pon* with the first discard of the Wind tile in cases where the hand has several pairs (two's of a kind), or adjoining tiles for sequences, or *Chi*(s), because, as explained before, we may be able to get some kind of Bonus. Whether to do so or not, depends upon one's ability which develops in due course of training.

Here is an example. Our hand is North, and East discards a South tile in the first round of play. If we make a *Pon* of South, a keen mind will guess that we have other Bonus tiles, so will not discard such Bonus tiles as the Green Dragon.

If the Eldest Hand, or East, has two tiles of East and two tiles of West, he should not make a *Pon* of the first discard of West. But he should make a *Pon* whenever an East tile is discarded, because that *Pon* will multiply his Fundamental Points by 4. He can do without the *Pon* of West because he loses only 4 points in that case.

If the Eldest Hand, or East, has one tile each of South, West and North, it is not easy to determine which tile should be discarded first. But to discard the Wind tile of the most lucky or the ablest hand, is the best policy.

CHAPTER II. HOW TO DEAL WITH 1-S AND 9-S OF THE NUMERAL TILES

After we discard the Wind tiles which do not make up Bonus *Pon* (s), we try to discard the 1-s and 9-s of the Numeral tiles, as they have less chance of making up sequences, or *Chi* (s), than the middle or intermediate Numeral tiles. When we seek to have a hand composed of Letter tiles and one kind of Numeral tiles, we should discard unnecessary 1-s and 9-s, prior to discarding Wind tiles. Often it happens that discarded 1-s and 9-s may be used by other hands later in the game in making a Pillow to Go Out.

We notice that the 1-s and 9-s and the Wind tiles are usually discarded in the early rounds of play. When they are not discarded in the early rounds, we must judge that someone is holding pairs of them.

CHAPTER III. HOW TO DEAL WITH THE BONUS TILES

Bonus tiles should be discarded carefully. Every player likes to have these tiles to make up many Bonuses. The *Pon* (s) of these Bonus tiles are actually not as valuable as beginners think. For instance, the Eldest Hand, in the East Round, has two East tiles and two Red Dragon tiles. An East tile is discarded, but the Eldest Hand does not take it to meld a Pon. He waits for a Red Dragon to be discarded. When a Red Dragon is discarded the Eldest Hand takes it to meld a *Pon*. Subsequently another East tile is discarded and the Eldest Hand Goes Out, melding the *Pon* of East. If the hand had melded a *Pon* with the first discard of the East tile, it would have served as a warning to the other hands, and they would not have discarded a Red Dragon tile because its *Pon* would give an added Bonus. At times, we can prepare our hands to Go Out after four or five turns of play. In this case we can often use a pair of Bonus tiles for a Pillow. When we wish to complete seven pairs, the 1-s and 9-s and the Letter tiles are the best to make up the Pillow. The Wind and Dragon tiles should not be discarded carelessly after several rounds of play, because someone is apt to be waiting to use these tiles to make up a Pillow, as stated above. This is true even though two of these tiles have been discarded. When we draw Bonus tiles near the end of the round of play it is better not to discard them, even though we give up the intention to Go Out.

This should be remembered.

Much has been stated about the Bonus tiles. However, an old Chinese proverb says, " Dragon tiles should not be discarded when one of each of these Dragon tiles are found at the first drawing but one should give up the intention to Go Out." Having one of each of the Dragon tiles is considered unlucky.

CHAPTER IV. RULES FOR THE MIDDLE OR INTERMEDIATE TILES

These middle or intermediate (2- to 8- Numeral) tiles are very convenient to use in arranging a hand to Go Out. At the same time they are also very useful to other hands. It sometimes happens, to our great regret, that we draw a 4-*Won* and a

5 *Won* after we have discarded a 6-*Won*. When we discard a 4- or a 6-Numeral tile, the right hand often uses it to make a *Chi*. That does not please us. We must investigate the right hand and try to prevent it from making a *Chi* or a *Pon*.

Since we cannot look at the hand we must judge it from our experiences. If we have a sequence of 2-*Won* and 3-*Won* in our hand, we need 1-*Won* or 4-*Won* to make up a *Chi*. If we have a 5-*Won* and a 6-*Won*, we need 4-*Won* or 7-*Won*. In reverse, 1-*Won* and 7-*Won* are not needed if 4-*Won* is not needed, except in case of *Pon* (s) of 1-*Won* and 7-*Won*. However, we cannot be certain that 4-*Won* or 7-*Won* are not needed, even if 1-*Won* is discarded. We call this the 1-4-7-Rule. Similarly, we have these Rules for 2 - 5 - 8 -, and for 3 - 6 - 9 -. These Rules are best remembered in making up <u>our</u> *Chi* (s) , and <u>not</u> to make up those of other hands.

When the right hand discards a 3-*Won* or a 2-*Won* early in the round, he discards it either out of a sequence of 1- 2- and 3-*Won*, or because it is a lone one. In case the hand has 3-3-4-*Won*, he discards the 3-*Won*. But this is not true at the first of the game. Then the discarded 2- or 3-*Won* must be a lone one. Therefore, the 1-*Won* is not dangerous. 2-*Won* can be discarded safely. When the 4-Bamboo is discarded by the right hand, the 1-Bamboo will not be picked up for a *Chi*, judging by the above Rules. But we cannot guess whether the hand will make a *Pon* or not. As for the 7-*Won*, it has a chance of being picked up to be used as an Intermediate between 6-*Won* and 8-*Won*, or as a Marginal of 8-*Won* and 9-*Won*. We can also apply this Rule to Going Out.

If a player has four or five pairs of one kind of successive Numeral tiles, he can Go Out by making *Chi* (s) or *Pon* (s). When one has three pairs of these successive Numeral tiles, he must think about the following tactics.

a.   5- and 6-, and 6- and 7-Numerals.

These are called " Stomach Swellers ".

You will probably wish to make two *Chi* (s) by combining these four tiles of 5- and 6-, and 6- and 7-. However, it does not follow that this is good strategy, except in the case when you " *Tempai* ", by making a *Chi* of one of these *Stomach Swellers*. " The word *TEMPAI* is very convenient to use, and moreover, very understandable. I propose that you use this word. It is both a noun and a verb, and means that the thirteen tiles in your hand are arranged, or ready, to Go Out."

In the above case, you can use a 4-, 5-, 6-, 7-, or an 8-Numeral. So you wait to draw one of these tiles from the pile, without making a *Chi* too hastily. Even if you do not draw one of these tiles from the pile, you may draw tiles which have connection with other tiles in your hand. Even when you draw one of the Bonus tiles, none of which is in your hand, you can console yourself that you have deprived the right hand player of getting it, and perhaps making a Bonus *Pon*.

You wait until you can pick these tiles from the pile. This Rule also applies to other cases, such as ; 1 - 2 - 2 - 3-, 2 - 3 - 3 - 4-, 3 - 4 - 4 - 5-, 4 - 5 - 5 - 6-, 6 - 7 - 7 - 8- and 7 - 8 - 8 - 9-.

b.   When one has successive fours, such as, 2 - 3 - 4 - 5-, you should not make a *Chi*. Even if a 1- or 3- is discarded you can often Go Out by making a Pillow of 2- or 5-. It is better strategy to wait and draw from the pile in this case also.

CHAPTER V.   *PON*

1.   It is one of the beginner's habits to make a *Pon* of 3-*Won*, when a 3-*Won* is discarded, if he is holding 1-*Won*, 2-*Won* and two 3-*Won*(s).   But you should not make a *Pon*.

You should keep the *Chi* of 1-2-3-*Won*. It is safe to discard your second 3-Won.

2. You can easily understand by the above, that you should not make a *Pon* of 6-*Won*, when you have 6-6-7-8-Won, and a 6-*Won* is discarded. However, you can do that, if you can *Tempai* by making the *Pon*, and wait for 6-*Won* or 9-*Won* to Go Out.

CHAPTER VI. TILES WHICH SHOULD BE DISCARDED

1. When you have 1- 4- and 7-Numerals in your hand, the 1-would be discarded first. Then you will wonder whether the 4- or the 7- should be discarded next. From the view point of combinations to make *Chi* (s), 4- has the same importance as 7-. But 7- is more valuable than 4- as a Marginal tile, for the player on the right may have an 8- and a 9-, and will be very glad to make a *Chi* of 7 - 8 - 9 - of the same Numeral.

2. 2- 5- and 8-

Generally speaking, the 2- is discarded first and the 8- next. Reversely speaking, since the 2- and the 8- are the tiles which are most apt to be discarded, one can often wait to pick up the discard and use it as an Intermediate tile. Sometimes it is wise to discard a 5- first and hold a 2- or an 8- to prevent them being picked up by the right hand player.

3. 3- 6- and 9-.

The 9- should be discarded first. The 3- must be dealt with like 7-. The old proverb says, " 3-s and 7-s are hard to get ". Such sequences as 1- and 2-, or 8- and 9-, should be discarded as soon as you draw other sequences such as 3- and 4-, or 5- and 6-.

4. 2-s and 8-s are easily discarded.

When your hand is *Tempai* (ed), you can wait for a 2- or an 8-, if you are holding 1- and 3-, or 7- and 9-.

As for strategy, we can strike when other players are absent-minded, or overly trusting of the Rules. We may discard a 5-Numeral and wait for a 2- or an 8-, or we may discard a 6- and wait to make up a *Pon* of 9-s, or use a 3- as a Marginal or an Intermediate tile.

However, we cannot be certain that a 5- will be discarded, even if we discard an 8-, as there are two combinations within the 2-5-8-Rule, which are 2- and 5-, and 5- and 8-.

In reverse, even if an 8- is a safe discard, there is another combination of 2- and 5-, and so 5- is not considered to be a safe discard.

CHAPTER VII. *TEMPAI*

When we have many Numeral tiles in our hand, we have many chances to Go Out. We can afford to wait, but often we wait and miss our chance for Going Out. Letting others Go Out with our discards is too regrettable to endure. From this point of view we must master these fundamental types of waiting.

One Chance

a. Going Out by making a Pillow.

For instance, we have one 1-*Won*, the other twelve tiles are arranged in sets of threes. We can Go Out by getting 1-*Won* to make up the Pillow. We may draw it from the pile or pick it up when it is discarded by another player.

b. Going Out with a Marginal tile.

If we have 1-2-Numerals, we wait for a 3-Numeral to make up a *Chi*.

If we have 8-9-Numerals, we wait for a 7-Numeral.

Two Chances

a. Fundamental type.

We have a sequence of two Numerals, such as 2-3-Numerals, so we wait for a 1- or a 4-Numeral, or we have a sequence of 5-6-Numerals and we wait for a 4- or a 7-Numeral.

b. Pillow and Marginal

If we have three 1-s and one 2-Numeral, we can Go Out by getting a 2- to make up a Pillow, or by getting a 3- for a Marginal tile to make a 1 - 2 - 3 - *Chi.*

If we have three 9-s and one 8-Numeral, we can Go Out by getting a 7- for a Marginal tile in a 7 - 8 - 9 - *Chi,* or an 8- to make up a Pillow.

c. The tile for Going Out.

We can apply the 1 - 4 - 7 -, the 2 - 5 - 8 - and the 3 - 6 - 9 - Rules, which were previously mentioned, for Going Out. Namely, we *Tempai* our hands, having two chances, waiting for such tiles as 1-, or 4- ; 2-, or 5- , etc., avoiding Pillows, or Intermediate, or Marginal tiles. Assuming that another hand *Tempai* (s) , we can guess what tile he wants, judging by his discards and appearances. When he discards a 4-Numeral, he does not have a 2- and 3-, or a 5- and 6-. This is easily deduced from the 1 - 4 - 7 - Rule. However, he may be waiting for a *Pon* of 1-s, or of 7-s, or he may want a 7- for an Intermediate or a Marginal tile.

When he discards a 1-, we should refrain from discarding a 7-. However, if we are holding two 8-Numerals and two other 8-s have been discarded, we know that he cannot be waiting to use a 7- as a Marginal tile. There are four tiles of each kind in the implements of play so we can often guess whether it is safe to discard, or not, judging from our hands and the tiles which have been discarded.

d. Pillow and Intermediate.

For instance, with three 4-s and one 2-, we can Go Out by getting a 2- to make up a Pillow, or, if we get a 3-Numeral, we can Go Out by using the 3- as an Intermediate to make a *Chi*, and use the other two 4-s as a Pillow. There are other examples, such as three 5-s and one 3- or one 7-, etc.

e. When we have a sequence of four tiles we have two chances to Go Out. For example, we have 4 - 5 - 6 - 7 -. We can Go Out by getting a 4- or a 7- for making a Pillow.

f. Pillows.

We have two 2-Bamboo tiles and two 7-Ball tiles. The other nine tiles are in sequences of threes. If we draw a 2-Bamboo, we can Go Out by making a *Pon* of the 2-Bamboo tiles and use the two 7-Ball tiles as the Pillow. In reverse, we can Go Out by making a *Pon* of the 7-Balls and the Pillow of the 2-Bamboo.

Three Chances

a. Fundamental type

A sequence of 2- to 6-Numerals (2 - 3 - 4 - 5 - 6 -) has three chances to Go Out, by getting a 1-, a 4-, or a 7-.

A sequence of 3- to 7-Numerals (3 - 4 - 5 - 6 - 7 -) can Go Out with a 2-, a 5-, or an 8-.

A sequence of 4- to 8-Numerals (4 - 5 - 6 - 7 - 8 -) can Go Out with a 3-, a 6-, or a 9-.

b. Three chances for a Pillow.

Sequences of 1- to 7-Numerals (1 - 2 - 3 - 4 - 5 - 6 - 7 -) have three chances to Go Out, by getting a 1-, or a 4-, or a 7-,

Sequences of 2- to 8-Numerals (2 - 3 - 4 - 5 - 6 - 7 - 8 -) can Go Out with a 2-, a 5-, or an 8-

Sequences of 3- to 9-Numerals (3 - 4 - 5- 6 - 7 - 8 - 9 -) can Go Out with a 3-, or a 6-, or a 9- for making up a Pillow.

c. Three of any Numeral from 3- to 7- and one adjoining tile.

For instance, a hand with three 3-s and one 2- (3 - 3 - 3 - 2 -), can wait for a 1-, or a 2- or a 4-. If he gets a 1-, or a 4- he makes a *Chi* and use the other two 3-s for a Pillow. If he draws or picks up a 2-, the two 2-s will make a Pillow and the three 3-s will be a concealed *Pon*.

d. Two of a kind and three of one kind of Numeral plus a sequence of two adjoining tiles.

For instance, two 3-s, three 6-s and a sequence of 7- 8-Numerals (3 - 3 - 6 - 6 - 6 - 7 - 8 -) can Go Out by getting a 3-, or a 6-, or a 9-. In cases like this, the two of a kind do not need to be limited to Numeral tiles only. That is, the two of a kind, which can be used as a Pillow or to make up a *Pon*, may be Letter tiles.

Four Chances

a. Hands such as the following have four chances to Go Out.

2 - 3 - 4 - 5 - 5 - 5 - 6 -.

3 - 4 - 5 - 6 - 6 - 6 - 7 -.

4 - 5 - 6 - 7 - 7 - 7 - 8 -.

In the first example, we wait for a 1-, a 4-, a 6-, or a 7-. If we get a 1-, or a 4-, or a 7- we make two *Chi*(s) and use the two 5-s as a Pillow. If we draw or pick up a 6-, we can Go Out by making the Pillow of 6-s.

b. Two of each of the 5-s and 6-s and three 7-s.

(5 - 5 - 6 - 6 - 7 - 7 - 7 -). In cases like this, we wait for a 5-, a 6-, a 4-, or a 7-.

Five Chances

a. One each of 2- to 5- and three 6-s (2 - 3 - 4 - 5 - 6 - 6 - 6 -).

One each of 3- to 6- and three 7-s (3 - 4 - 5 - 6 - 7 - 7 - 7 -).

One each of 4- to 7- and three 8-s (4 - 5 - 6 - 7 - 8 - 8 - 8 -).

In the first example, we can Go Out with a 1-, or a 4-, or a 7-, and use the two 6-s for a Pillow. Furthermore, we can Go Out by drawing either a 2- or a 5- to make up a Pillow. So we have five chances to Go Out.

b. Three 3-s and three 5-s and one 4- (3 - 3 - 3 - 4 - 5 - 5 - 5 -).

There is a *Chi* of 3 - 4 - 5 -. If we draw a 3- or a 5-, we can Go Out by making a Pillow of one and using the other as a concealed *Pon*. If we draw a 4-, we make a Pillow of the two 4-s, and Go Out with two concealed *Pons* of 3-s and 5-s. If we draw a 6- or a 2-, we can Go Out with a *Chi*, a *Pon* and a Pillow of either 3-s or 5-s. Therefore, we have five chances to Go Out with a 2-, a 3-, a 4-, a 5-, or a 6-. We must take care that some other player does not have the same chance.

Six Chances

a. Three 2-s and three 3-s and one each of 4- to 7-,
(2 - 2 - 2 - 3 - 3 - 3- 4 - 5 - 6 - 7 -)

If we use 2 - 3 - 4 - and 5 - 6 - 7 - as two *Chi*(s), we can Go Out with a fourth 2- or 3-, making a *Pon* of one and a Pillow of the other 2-s or 3-s.

If we treat the three 2-s and the three 3-s as two *Pon*(s) we can wait for a 4- or a 7- to make up a Pillow.

If the three 2-s are assumed to be a *Pon* and two of the 3-s a Pillow, we can wait for a 2-, or a 5-, or an 8-.

Therefore, we have six chances to Go Out with a 2-, a 3-, a 4-, a 5-, a 7-, or an 8-.

This happens in other cases, such as, with three 1-s and three 2-s and one each of 3- to 6-, 1 - 1 - 1 - 2 - 2 - 2 - 3 - 4 - 5 - 6 -, and with 3 - 3 - 3 - 4 - 4 - 4 - 5 - 6 - 7 - 8 -.

b. The following hand also has six chances to Go Out.
2 - 2 - 2 - 3 - 4 - 5 - 6 - 7 - 8 - 9 -.

When the three 2-s are treated as a *Pon*, we can wait for a 3-, a 6-, or a 9- to make up a Pillow. If two of the 2-s are used as a Pillow, we can wait for a 1-, or a 4-, or a 7- to make up three *Chi*(s).

Seven Chances

Hands, such as the following have seven chances to Go Out. Two sets of three of a kind and an intermediate sequence of four Numerals, 1 - 1 - 1 - 2 - 3 - 4 - 5 - 6 - 6 - 6-, or 4 - 4 - 4 - 5 - 6 - 7 - 8 - 9 - 9 - 9 -.

These hands can Go Out with a 1-, a 2-, a 3-, a 4-, a 5-, a 6-, or a 7-, in the first case, and with a 3-, a 4-, a 5-, 6-, 7-, an 8-, or a 9-. in the second.

Eight Chances

Hands like the following have eight chances to Go Out. A hand with 2 - 2 - 2 - 3 - 4 - 5 - 6 - 7 - 7 - 7 - can Go Out with a 1-, a 2-, a 3-, a 4-, a 5-, a 6-, a 7-, or an 8-.

A hand with 3 - 3 - 3 - 4 - 5 - 6 - 7 - 8- 8 - 8 - can Go Out with a 2-, a 3-, a 4-, a 5-, a 6-, a 7-, an 8-, or a 9-.

Nine Chances

This hand is illustrated in the previous chapter on Maximum Points. 1 - 1 - 1 - 2 - 3 - 4 - 5 - 6 - 7 - 8 - 9 - 9 - 9 -.

CHAPTER VIII. HOW TO MAKE *TEMPAI*

Various types of *Tempai* were explained in the last Chapter. However, it sometimes happens that a hand with only one chance will Go Out, even if others have several chances for Going Out. This is due to the fact that the chances for Going Out do not depend entirely on the composition of the hand and the strategy of play.

Every hand has 13 or 14 tiles. Many tiles are discarded, moreover, the drawing of tiles from the pile must not be forgotten. When four tiles of one kind have been discarded, there naturally is no further chance to wait for one of those tiles, but until that time there is always the chance that the tile one waits for may be discarded by one of the other players, or it may still be drawn from the pile.

Therefore, we must be aware that the real element of chance enters into the playing of Mah Jong, and take this into account. This element is apparent when, many times, most of the pile will be eaten up by many drawings, before even a good hand with many chances for Going Out attains sucess.

Drawing constantly changes the hand and a safe tile in one round of play may not always be a safe tile to discard in the next turn of play. To guess whether a tile is safe to discard, or not, is very difficult. Consultation of discarded tiles is a great help and the applying of the Rules of 1- 4- 7-, and 2- 5- 8-, etc. The following are examples.

a. A hand has three complete sets of three and a Pillow, the remaining tiles are 5-Ball, 3-Ball and 1-Ball. To *Tempai*, we must discard one of the three. So far neither a 2-Ball, nor a 5-Ball has been discarded, but a 1-Ball and a 4-Ball have been discarded. To wait for the discarding of a 4-Ball is the ordinary method, discarding the 1-Ball. However, sometimes discarding the 5-Ball may be successful, if one thinks the other players might overtrust the 2- 5- 8- Rule.

b. Having 9- 7- 7- 6- of any Numeral, we will make a *Pon* of 7-s, when a 7- is discarded, then discard the 6- and wait for another 9- to make a Pillow. 9-s are more often discarded because of the 3- 6- 9- Rule. For the some reason, having 2- 3- 3-, or 7- 7- 8- we should wait for a 2- or an 8-, after we have made a *Pon* of the 3-s or the 7-s. Numeral tiles from

3- to 7- are valuable and should be kept in the hand for a long time. Those tiles, which are valuable to you, are at the same time valuable to others. Often a hand is betrayed by discarding one of these valuable tiles, in order to *Tempai*, because some other hand may use it to Go Out.

c. This hand has 1- 1- 4- 5- 5- 3- 3-. All do not need to be the same kind of Numeral (the two 1-s and 3-s may be Letter tiles), but the 4- 5- 5- must be the same. The other six tiles in the hand are arranged in two sets of threes. This is a good hand to wait for *Tempai*. If a 1-, a 5-, or a 3- is discarded, we can make a *Pon*. If a 5- is discarded, we *Tempai*, waiting for a 1- or a 3- for a *Pon* and a Pillow. But if a 1- or a 3- is discarded and we make a *Pon*, it is better to discard a 5-, not the 4-. In this case, we give up the chance to make a *Pon* of 5-s and wait to make a *Chi* with a 3- or a 6-. We call this *Tempai*-adjoining *Tempai*.

When the above hand is completed, it is good strategy to discard one of the 5-s at once. Discarding the 5- early is better for two reasons : first, it is safe, because the 5- is a valuable tile, and second, the other players will scarcely suspect a *Tempai*.

CHAPTER IX. *FURI TEM*-GOING OUT WITH A DISCARDED TILE

We often notice that the tile we need to Go Out is one we have discarded early in the game as being unnecessary. When this occurs and our hand is ready to *Tempai*, we must declare the situation by saying, " *Furi Tem* ". *Furi Tem* is Chinese for Sacred Discard.

For instance, we discarded a 9-Ball because at first, it had no connection with the other tiles in our hand. After several drawings, we obtain a 7-Ball and an 8-Ball and can *Tempai*,

At this time we must make the declaration that we can Go Out by a tile which we ourselves have previously discarded. We do not name the tile, but the other hands are warned when we say "*Furi Tem*", and are careful in making discards. The declaration depends upon the type of hand that is held. Having 2 - 3 - 4 - 5 - 6 - in our hand, we wait for a 1-, or a 7-. If we have discarded a 1-, or a 4-, or a 7- and wish to use one of the same Numerals discarded by one of the other players to Go Out, we must declare "*Furi Tem*".

If we do not make the declaration and should Go Out by picking up the same tile that we have already discarded when it is discarded by another, we must pay half of the Maximum points as a penalty.

To Avoid Making the Declaration.

Using the above hand as an example. If a player has discarded a 1-Numeral he can avoid making the declaration if he waits only for a 4- or a 7-. In the same way, if he has discarded a 7-Numeral, he does not need to declare "*Furi Tem*", if he Goes Out with a 1- or a 4-.

But if he has discarded a 4-Numeral, he must make the declaration, even though he may Go Out, by using a discarded 1-, or 7-, or 4-.

However, one can Go Out, unquestionably, by drawing from the pile. If a player desires to Go Out by drawing from the pile, he does not need to make the declaration of "*Furi Tem*".

CHAPTER X.   REN-CHON

When the Eldest Hand, or East, Goes Out, it plays again as the East hand, and the game is called *Ren-chon*. Players use different rules concerning *Ren-chon*.

1.   After the first game, the hand that Goes Out must have

at least one Bonus. Namely, the Bonuses are the qualifications for Going Out.

2.   a. At the beginning of a *Ren-chon*, every hand puts forward (antes, or places on the table) 100 points, which are given to the winner of the game. If East wins a second *Ren-chon*, the players each put forward 200 points. On the third *Ren-chon*, the players ante 300 points each. At the beginning of the first *Ren-chon*, the Eldest Hand, or East, places a 10-point counting bar on the table to his right. If he wins, he places two 10-point counting bars on the table for the next game. Thus the number increases according to the number of *Ren-chons*. (These bars serve as counters only).

b.   At the end of the first *Ren-chon*, if the winner Goes Out with a discarded tile, the one who discarded pays the winner an extra 300 points (100 points for each of the other three players). In the second *Ren-chon*, the winner is paid 600 points. However, this rule is esteemed to be too burdensome for the one who discarded, so if the winner Goes Out with a discarded tile, the one who discarded pays only his own share as the extra points, namely, 100 points in the first *Ren-chon*, 200 points in the second, and so on.

In every case, when the winner Goes Out by drawing from the pile, the other three players pay their own share, that is, 100 points each for the first *Ren-chon*, 200 for the second, etc.

SUPPLEMENTARY

In previous Chapters we have shown the most fundamental rules and methods of play as translated from the official Japanese book of rules for Mah Jong. Counting the points by those rules is an intricate process and many players prefer to use an easier system of counting and a simplified way of casting dice. In the following paragraphs we shall reveal those rules and regulations in popular use.

1. *Casting Dice*

After the seats of the four players are decided by casting the dice twice, we simplify the throwing of the dice by casting only once instead of twice.

For instance, the Eldest Hand, or East, throws the dice and, at once, starts the game by taking four tiles from the place indicated by the number of spots on the dice. Namely, when the spots on the dice add up to seven, he takes the four tiles from West's pile (having counted round the table, starting with himself, to seven), excluding *seven* piles from the right end of West's pile. Every round of play begins in like manner.

Before starting the game, the four players must decide whether the dice shall be thrown once or twice.

2. *Bonus Regulations*

Recently people in Japan have suffered from the heavy burden of inflation and a majority of Mah Jong players thought the counting system according to the old rules did not have sufficient multiplication. This demand was met by the following higher Bonus system, which is favored by most present day players.

The following Bonuses have been added to the Fundamental System. Those not referred to remain unchanged.

Hands which Go Out with the following :—

a. All *Pon* (s) .... F. P. × 4 (before × 2)

b, Letter tiles and Numeral tiles............F. P. × 4 (before × 2)

c. Only ONE kind of Numeral............F. P. × 16 (before × 8)

d. Three concealed *Pon* (s) ....F. P. × 4 (before × 2)

e. Complete concealed Sequence of 1-Numeral to 9-Numeral (same kind) ....F. P. × 4

If one or more *Chi*(s) in the above hand are melded, as for instance, a 4-5-6 *Chi*, the points are doubled......F. P. × 2

Before, both concealed and melded *Chi*(s) were treated the same and doubled.

f. If a hand has the same *Chi*(s) in three Numerals, as, for instance, 3-4-5-*Won*, 3-4-5-Bamboo and 3-4-5-Balls, the points are doubled ....F. P. × 2

g. This also happens in the case of three *Pon*(s) of the three Numerals. For instance, if a hand has *Pon*(s) of 5-Balls, 5-Bamboo and 5-*Won* the points are doubled......F. P. × 2

h. In a hand having Numeral and Letter tiles, if ALL the Numeral *Chi*(s) or *Pon*(s) include 1-s or 9-s, the points are doubled...F. P. × 2

For example, 1-1-1-Bamboo, 1-2-3-*Won*, 7-8-9-Balls, a *Pon* of Red Dragons and a Pillow of Letter tiles ....F. P. × 2

i. However, if a hand has Numeral tiles ONLY, and every *Chi* or *Pon* includes a 1- or a 9-Numeral, then the points are multiplied by four .... F. P. × 4

For examyle, 9-9-9-*Won*, 7-8-9-*Won*, 1-2-3-Balls, 1-1-1-*Won* and a Pillow of 9-Bamboo.................................F. P. × 4

j. Two *Pon*(s) of Dragon tiles and a Pillow of Dragon tiles .... F. P. × 4

Formerly the F. P. were only doubled.

k. Seven Pairs. When the seven pairs are all middle tiles (no 1-s or 9-s) ....F. P. × 2

If the seven pairs are composed of Letter tiles and only

ONE kind of Numeral .... F. P. × 4

If the seven pairs are composed of ONE kind of Numeral tiles ONLY...F. P. × 16

In the case of seven pairs the Rule of *Rhichi* which will be referred to later, can be used.

Rules set forth in f., g. and h. have only recently been introduced and have not been presented before. Many new rules are being used but many are not considered acceptable. Only those, which have been carefully tested and found to be good, are shown here.

Before starting to play, the players should have a conference about what rules and regulations will be applied to the game.

3. *Counting*

Even if we use the Bonus Rules which are referred to in paragraph 2., we do not need to change the counting system. However, some people are bothered by the old intricate counting system and have initiated a new system.

When the Fundamental Points are 22, they are raised to 30, then the 30 points are multiplied, according to the Bonus Rules.

4. *Rhichi*

The rule of *Rhichi* was not recommended before, but it is usually used by present day players. As soon as our hand is *Tempai*(ed) (ready to Go Out except for one tile), we declare *Rhichi*. Though we cannot change our hand after the declaration by drawing or by making a *Pon* or a *Chi*, if we Go Out the Fundamental Points are doubled.

When a player declares *Rhichi*, he puts forward 100 points. If he wins, he takes it back, but if another hand Goes Out, he must present the 100 points to the winner.

The End.

The rule of *Rhichi* was not recommended before, but it is usually used by present day players. As soon as our hand is *Tempai*(ed) (ready to Go Out except for one tile), we declare *Rhichi*. Though we cannot change our hand after the declaration by drawing or by making a *Pon* or a *Chi*, if we Go Out the Fundamental Points are doubled.

When a player declares *Rhichi*, he puts forward 100 points. If he wins, he takes it back, but if another hand Goes Out, he must present the 100 points to the winner.

5. *Irregular Playing with Three Persons*

In the course of playing Mah Jong, it sometimes happens that only three persons can meet together. Although less interesting than a four handed game, three persons can play as follows

The three hands are East, South, and West. There is no North. The tiles of North are treated as Bonus tiles, the same as Dragon tiles. One game has only three rounds of play—East, South, and West—instead of the normal four.

6. *Irregular Playing with Five Persons*

One of each of the four Wind tiles and a White Dragon tile are shuffled upside down on the table. Each person takes a tile. The four players who draw Wind tiles take seats at the table and play according to the usual rules. The fifth player, who drew the White Dragon tile, is excluded from the first game of the East Round. However, each of the five players has counting bars valued at 2,000 points.

At the second hand of the East Round, the South of the last turn becomes East, and East gives up his seat to the White Dragon, who brings his own counting bars. This is the North hand. At the third hand, the East of the first hand becomes North, and the South of the first hand or the East of the second is excluded from the play. Thus the game continues, with each player being excluded in turn, to the end of the North.

7. *Tournament Play*

In tournaments a way must be devised whereby the same persons do not continue playing at the same tables. Less than four tables present no great problem, and we shall describe the system for four tables or more.

In the following tabulations capital letters indicate the table, and Arabic numerals indicate each individual player, each table and player keeping the same designation throughout the tournament.

Four Tables, Sixteen Persons

	1st Play	2nd Play	3rd Play	4th Play
A.	1, 5, 9, 13	1, 6, 11, 16	1, 7, 12, 14	1, 8, 10, 15
B.	2, 6, 10, 14	2, 5, 12, 15	2, 8, 11, 13	2, 7, 9, 16
C.	3, 7, 11, 15	3, 8, 9, 14	3, 5, 10, 16	3, 6, 12, 13
D.	4, 8, 12, 16	4, 7, 10, 13	4, 6, 9, 15	4, 5, 11, 14

Five Tables, Twenty Persons

A.	1, 6, 11, 16	1, 10, 19, 8	1, 14, 7, 20	1, 18, 15, 12
B.	5, 10, 15, 20	5, 14, 3, 12	5, 18, 11, 4	5, 2, 19, 16
C.	9, 14, 19, 4	9, 18, 7, 16	9, 2, 15, 8	9, 6, 3, 20
D.	13, 18, 3, 8	13, 2, 11, 20	13, 6, 19, 12	13, 10, 7, 4
E.	17, 2, 7, 12	17, 6, 15, 4	17, 10, 3, 16	17, 14, 11, 8

Six Tables, Twenty-four Persons

A.	1, 6, 11, 16	1, 10, 19, 4	1, 14, 7, 20	1, 18, 15, 8
B.	5, 10, 15, 20	5, 14, 23, 8	5, 18, 11, 24	5, 22, 19, 12
C.	9, 14, 19, 24	9, 18, 3, 12	9, 22, 15, 4	9, 2, 23, 16
D.	13, 18, 23, 4	13, 22, 7, 16	13, 2, 19, 5	13, 6, 3, 20
E.	17, 22, 3, 8	17, 2, 11, 20	17, 6, 23, 12	17, 10, 7, 24
F.	21, 2, 7, 12	21, 6, 15, 24	21, 10, 3, 16	21, 14, 11, 4